SOMETHING TO SMILE ABOUT

Pam Quinn

GW00703037

ARTHUR H. STOCKWELL LTD
Torrs Park   Ilfracombe   Devon
Established 1898
www.ahstockwell.co.uk

British Library Cataloguing-in-Publication Data.
A catalogue record for this book is available
from the British Library.

Some names and circumstances have been changed
for reasons of confidentiality.

ISBN 978-0-7223-3901-5
Printed in Great Britain by
Arthur H. Stockwell Ltd
Torrs Park   Ilfracombe
Devon

CONTENTS

About the Author

Being the eldest of five,
I happily spent my early life
Looking after younger children –
Both mine and the neighbours –
Followed by working in children's homes.

Then later on began my love for
The 'Hostel Ladies' whilst I was
An officer in the Salvation Army –
But am I painting too rosy a picture?

Well, my life is just like the next bloke's,
With downs as well as ups;
It's not how often you fall that counts,
But whether or not you get up again.

Like the time when I had to escape
From a man in a railway carriage!
The experience left me very nervous,
But all the more able to assist other nervous folk.

The times when I was ill,
Which led up to my resignation –
It means that I am no longer found with the masses,
But that I revel in looking after the ones and twos.

I often quote, "As the Good Book says . . ."
But God, the Author, is a major part of my life too.

Watch out! Pam Writes Books

It was supposed to be a harmless game
Of Trivial Pursuit;
We played it on one of our 'signing nights'
At the Adult Learning Centre,
But during the game
We had a history and geography lesson,
And (quite by mistake)
A sex lesson!
And some swear signs too.

Now I don't write about rude things,
But I'm quite happy for you
To use your imagination about the latter.
So this is how it went:

"That's not the sign for juggling,
That means – – – – – – – – – !
That's not the sign for bus,
That means – – – – !
That's not the right sign,
That means prostitute!
I think that's when our tutor said,
"Watch out! Pam writes books."

But I was too busy remembering a time
When I thought I'd used the sign for 'alone'
Only to be stopped and told,
"Pam, that's the sign for condom!"
And it was suggested that I join
The Family Planning Clinic
As an adviser!

It really is surprising what you learn
At the
Adult Learning Centre
On a 'signing night'!

Mrs B

There I stood at the top of the steps,
Furiously putting up curtain hooks again
For the hostel cubicle curtains.
"I really don't know what keeps happening
To these curtain hooks," I loudly complained.

To my surprise, back came the answer:
"It doesn't matter what sort of tin-opener you use,
You'll still find baked beans inside the can."
Mrs B stated, in a matter-of-fact sort of voice,
"What? Pardon? Whatever did she mean?"
Her answer needed some thinking about;
But then I remembered that Mrs B
Was a research scientist,
And being on her wavelength helped me understand.

But having the answers to such questions
Wasn't the only thing you could credit Mrs B for;
For she helped out on a Sunday, also,
By playing the piano during the service.

Mind you, you couldn't take her for granted,
For Mrs B didn't sit at the piano;
No, she sat right at the back of the hall
And you just sort of hoped that she'd play her part.

The thing to do was to announce the song,
And, with a little bit of faith, begin to sing;
Then, if Mrs B knew the tune,
She'd walk from the back and sit and play for you
Only to return to her seat again
Once the song was over.
Then the person who was leading
Suggested and began to sing again –
Hopeful that Mrs B
Would oblige once again –
And breathe a heartfelt prayer:
"Thank you, Lord, for Mrs B."

A Wicked Sense of Humour

Pixie and I sat in A & E.
She was a little dot of a thing
With a wicked sense of humour
Who had injured her arm.

A man entered the waiting room.
"Put your hand on your halfpenny,"
She shouted out loud;
But none of us moved.

Pixie put her hand in the appropriate place,
And gave the command again.
"Put your hand on your halfpenny;
You can't trust a man an inch."

She looked steadily at me
Until I obediently put
My hand onto the correct place!
But she still wasn't satisfied.

She eyed the other females in the room
And said again, "Put your hand on your halfpenny."
The embarrassed man got up and left,
And Pixie and I were thankfully
Taken into the X-ray department.

What a Clever Mum!

I was in a crowded Tube station
When I saw her and her mum.
The little girl was in a bright-yellow mac,
Holding hands they boarded the Tube.

They were surrounded by other passengers,
But the little girl, dressed in bright yellow,
Could be seen by one and all.
Nobody would bump into her.

But her clever mum had gone one step further,
For on the back of the bright-yellow mac
Was written these words:
'Be Careful – Little Kid
In Big Yellow Mac'.

Halfway There

In Sunday school we were learning
About the Ten Commandments,
And we had reached the one that says,
'Thou shalt not steal'.

So I said to my class,
Who were all aged between three and five years,
"Why should you never take
Anything that doesn't belong to you?"

Only one of them tried an answer –
It was our then three-year-old,
And I reckon she was half way there:
"Because you will get a turn later on,"
Grace proudly shared with us.

A Little Girl's Prayer

At seven weeks the unborn baby died;
The longed-for new life was lost
And there was much sadness
Both in the family and the church.

In Sunday school that morning
Little Grace prayed so sincerely.
Her arms covered her face as she said,
"Dear Jesus, my mummy's not very well –
Please make her better.
Our Rosie has died –
Please look after her. Amen."

Now I really thought that Rosie
Must have been the name
Given to the unborn baby.

The next day I shared
The prayer with her dad.
"Oh no," said her dad,
"She's not still praying for Rosie!
Rosie was her rabbit
That died six months ago!"

A Young Gentleman

Jack held my hand as we got on the bus;
Every seat had just one person on it.
I sat beside a lady, and said to Jack,
"Why don't you sit by this man?"

Jack was feeling rather shy;
He shook his head and stood in the aisle.
That was when an elderly lady got on the bus;
"You are a nice young gentleman," she told Jack,
"Letting me have your seat."
Jack just beamed for the rest of the journey.

A Broken Window

We were standing waiting for a bus;
Jack was most concerned about a broken window.
"Who did that?" he signed to me.
"It must have been the big boys," I answered.

Then a man came, that we knew well.
"My, you are getting big," he told Jack.
Quick as a flash, Jack was hiding behind me.
"What's the matter?" I asked.

"I'm not big," he signed to me.
Light dawned, and I said,
"It's OK, I know you didn't break the window;
You're not in any trouble,"
Before I then explained to the man.

A Square Peg

Can a square peg
Fit into a round hole?
Of course not,
I hear you say;
But I have proof otherwise.

We sat on the bus, Jack and I,
Overlooking the waiting Euro train;
It was waiting to go into the tunnel.
"That's the Euro train,"
I informed my young friend.

"It's waiting to go into the tunnel."
"It not fit!" he replied.
I looked down at the sight –
I could see what he meant.

The front of the train was square,
Whilst the tunnel entrance was round!
But it did fit:
We watched it disappear!

Which just goes to show
That there's hope
For all of us square pegs!

Big Boys

It was my morning
To look after the under-fives;
A couple of them had colds
(And one of my pet hates
Is a runny nose – ugh!).

So I set about teaching them
How to use a tissue,
And where to keep your tissue.
Only a couple had pockets,
So others needed to put them
Up their sleeves.

They didn't think much
To "Keep it up your sleeves,"
So finally I said,
"This makes you look like
The big boys – with muscles!"

Their eyes lit up and they chuckled
As they pushed their tissues
Up their sleeves;
And then the doorbell rang.

Off ran one of our little boys.
Thankfully the visitor was most amused
When he heard,
"Look, I've got a bum on my arm!"

Jack Liked Buses

I've two memories of us sitting at the front;
Both were a little embarrassing,
But now I look back on them fondly
For memories of children growing up are always special.

The first is of him sitting there
Practising his talking –
The bus drivers adored him,
And he always left with sweets.

In those days Jack liked to shout;
And so he'd begin:
"Left" followed by "Turn".
The second word came much later.

Then came "Right" and . . . "Turn",
But the worst bit was when
He shouted, "CRASH . . . NOW!"
Much to everyone's amusement.

On the other occasion, we had to move.
As we sat down I told him,
"If an old lady, or an old man,
Or somebody who doesn't walk properly,
Gets on, we will have to move."

At the next stop, a teenager got on.
"Is that a old man?" he asked.
I shook my head as I said "Sorry"
To the boy concerned.

He was followed by a mum,
And her toddler, at which I was asked,
"That a old lady?" "No," I said.
Then came the third person.

This man was black and agile,
But, to my amazement, Jack asked,
"That a body that can't walk?"
I said "Sorry" to the man.

And then to Jack I said,
"Come on, we're moving to the back!"

Honest Hannah

The children played a team game
One Friday night at club.
"Stand in the hoopla ring,
Pull it up and over your head,
Then put the beanbag on your head.
Walk quickly to, and throw it
Into the rubber ring," they were told.

The teams were of mixed ages,
But all between five and eleven years,
Boys and girls sitting in four teams,
Listening as the game was explained.
All was prepared and the game began.

Hannah's team was running level
With the others when disaster struck.
Into the hoopla hoop stepped Hannah;
Up and over her head it went;
She picked up the beanbag and
Ran to that waiting rubber ring.

Nearly there when she remembered
The beanbag was still in her hand –
She had forgotten to put it on her head.
Back went Hannah to the beginning.
The rest of team gasped!
Now their team was running behind the others.

The beanbag was now on her head
And Hannah set off again,
Threw the beanbag into the rubber ring
And off went the next team member.
Of course, as was expected,
Hannah's team came in last.

The team points were awarded:
400 for the first team
And 300 for the second,
200 for the second to last
And just 100 for Hannah's team –
As was to be expected.

But what was this the leader was saying?
"I saw Hannah's honesty:
When Hannah realised that she had forgotten
To put the beanbag on her head
She went back to the beginning.
Because Hannah didn't cheat,
But started again, her team –
Gets another 100 points!"

Which meant that their team
Didn't come last after all,
But joint third, and that only goes to prove
That being honest is best!

I'm Better Now

It was the week that led up to Easter,
And a little girl in our church
Was wandering around close to tears;
And we just could not console her.

"What's the matter? Why so sad?"
"Jesus is dead," came the reply.
"But on Sunday he will be alive again,"
We tried to reassure her.

But she would not be consoled,
And all that week she wore her worried face.
For her it was the now that mattered.
It's difficult for a three-year-old to understand
The promised hope for tomorrow.

But then came Easter Sunday,
And in she came with a great big smile.
"I'm better now," she announced;
"Jesus is alive again!"

And in my heart I whispered,
"Thank you, Jesus."

Little Gems

A Word to the Wise

As I sat behind them I overheard:
"And as you get older you'll find
That you can catch a ball more easily,"
Said seven-year-old Hannah
To four-year-old Grace.

Setting an Example

I stood in the church hallway, nursing a cup of tea,
Chatting with other adults.
The children had been good
Throughout the church meeting;
Now they were letting off steam.
We turned a blind eye as two
Of the big boys raced past us;
Then two-year-old Adam
Followed, drew level and stopped.
"Excuse me, Pam," he said
Before carrying on his way.

Credit Indeed!

JACK: I support Man U. What team do you support?
JOEL: Tottenham Hotspur.
JACK: I suppose they could be a good team really.

"Jack, did you hear that Joel has been named Choirboy of the Year?"
"You tell him he did good!"

The Marble Slabs

At the Salvation Army Training College,
They were getting ready for the arrival of new cadets.
And one of the things that meant was
Getting twenty marble slabs into their bedrooms.

That meant twenty marble slabs
Carried down three flights of stairs,
Across the Quad,
And up three more flights of stairs.

They'd managed it fifteen times
Before they saw the notice left by a previous cadet.
Hanging on the bedroom door handle
Were the words 'Hallelujah Anyway'!

That was just the encouragement they needed;
This was something to smile about.
'Only five more to go,' they thought
As they breathed a sigh of relief.

The Pigs

I remember visiting some pigs
When my sister and I were quite young.
There were several of them
Kept behind a wire fence.

We would hide around the corner,
Jump out and shout, "Boo!"
The pigs, although unhurt,
Would run away squealing.

Time and again we'd hide
And then shout, "Boo!"
And every time they'd run
Squealing in fright.

Today, on my mantelshelf,
I have a large postcard. It reads,
'Nothing in this world is to be feared –
Only to be understood.'

Now that I'm a grown-up,
I appreciate this truth:
When I feel like squealing, although unhurt,
I don't run away, as did the pigs.

When something or someone shouts at me,
I take a big breath and bravely face it –
Even this wayward computer!

You Want Pig?

We'd just got in from school,
And I asked the usual question:
"What would you like to eat?"
Using her sign language,
Abigail signed "pig".

"You want pig?" I asked,
Suspicious that I'd got it wrong,
For communicating with Abi
Is far from easy.

I suggested a ham sandwich,
But still she signed "pig".
I offered a bacon roll,
But still she signed "pig".

Finally I said, "I don't know
What it is that you want."
Abigail ran screaming from the room
Into my bedroom and onto the bed.

Face down, she sobbed and sobbed.
I tried to comfort her;
"Way! Way! Way!" she shouted,
And I did as I was bid.

It was obvious that she'd had a bad day;
I would have to tread carefully.
Distraction must be the answer –
It was, and it worked!

Teletubbies was played loudly on the video;
Biscuits and juice were placed on the table;
Then, with my gaze on the TV, I waited.
I didn't have to wait long.

Out of the corner of my eye, I saw her.
Kneeling at the table, she consumed her little feast;
Then she crawled across and climbed on my lap.
"I'm sorry," she signed.
"I'm sorry too," I signed and said,
And we settled down together, watching *Teletubbies*.
Later on in the week, I phoned her mum.

"What does the 'pig' sign mean?" I asked.
"It stands for 'piggy biscuits'," she said.
"And just what" I asked "are 'piggy biscuits'?"
"Fig rolls," came back the answer.
Well, I would never have guessed.

The next week I earned my Brownie points.
As we stood waiting for the bus
I produced 'piggy biscuits' and juice.
I was rewarded with a signed
"Thank you, thank you, thank you"
And several cuddles as she jumped up and down
Before she began to tuck in.

And Martin Got Lost

There we were
At Clitheroe Castle Fête –
Myself and eight children,
All dressed in red tee shirts.

We were all having a good time,
The children and I,
Between the ices and the rides;
But then Martin wandered off!

"I'm sorry," I told the other children,
"But we'll all have to wait here
Till Martin gets back."
Glum faces were my answer.

Then a man with a monkey appeared,
And delightedly we surrounded the monkey;
And whilst Martin's name was boomed out
We had our photo taken.

We had our photo and I parted with the money,
And just as the man was leaving
Martin appeared in the Lost Children's Tent.
"We had our photo taken," he was told.

Our youngest child grinned at Martin.
Martin thought he should have his taken too,
But the man, his camera and the monkey
Had all gone from the fête.

When our youngest repeated,
"We had our photo taken with a monkey,"
Martin looked like he would murder him;
And I said, "That's enough."

Martin smiled – that was him told!
The youngest was close to tears,
But I reckoned that it was better than murder;
"Come on," I said. "Let's get an ice cream,"
And amidst the smiles we made our way home.

Martin and the Cat

Twelve-year-old Martin
Had thick-lens glasses,
Looked like a professor,
And always had his head in a book.

He was an absolute loner,
But all that changed
When he brought home a cat.
It must have belonged to someone.

But the Boss said he could keep it
Until someone else claimed it.
He'd have to look after it –
Even spend his pocket money.
And all this was agreed on.

Now I have to explain: I hate cats!
I have some sort of phobia,
And, like all true phobias,
I'm scared beyond belief – of cats!

So I took Martin to one side.
He promised he'd keep it away;
He'd shut it in his bedroom;
It need never come near me.

Then came the day that it got out;
Followed him all the way to school;
Sat and watched him all that day
Through the windowpane.

It followed him home again,
Where they were joined by our new girl.
Martin and the cat befriended her
And she became known as Kitty.

A few days later, the cat disappeared;
It was away for three days.
When it appeared with another cat,
"Sorry," said the Boss, "you can't keep two."

"It's OK," Martin assured her;
"Now that the cat has a friend
He can manage without me.
I'll take them both to the pet shop."

"But won't you be lonely?"
"No, I've got Kitty for a friend."
And that's just how it was:
Friends because of a lost cat.

And I'm So Proud

My friend Jack
Came to our beach party yesterday,
And I'm so proud of him.
Gone is the little boy
Who buried his face in my chest
If anyone looked his way.

Now he's sixteen going on seventeen,
But I remember when
He was six going on seven,
Struggling to learn to put words into sentences,
Struggling to learn things that other children
Did by instinct.
But now he can hold a conversation
And has overcome so many difficulties.

Yesterday I watched,
Reflected and remembered;
The child that I helped now helps me.
When I get stuck, he helps me up.
He comes with his strimmer,
Mows my lawn,
And then goes round the edges,
Keeping my garden in order.

Yesterday I watched –
Oh, so proudly.
Now he has the courage to play with others.
Gone is the little boy who sat beside me,
Watching whilst others played.

Nowadays he is the proud possessor
Of a mobile phone,
And uses it with expert ease.
Like other teenagers,
He does things that I as a grown-up
Haven't yet learnt how to do.

One more week at school,
Then next term it's college.
And I'm so proud of him –
So proud of this young gentleman,
Taking his place in the big wide world
With such confidence.

God bless him and watch over him
As he makes his mark in the world.

Nappies

That's right – nappies.
I was a big girl of six
And I had to wear
My brother's nappy!

I still remember the indignation!
I'd had a lovely swim
In the crowded baths;
But that 'lovely' changed to 'Oh no!'

The changing rooms were communal,
And when I went to change
Someone had pinched my pants!
So, in just my dress and shoes,
I went to find my mum.

"Somebody's pinched my pants,"
I explained to her.
Back came the answer:
"You'll have to wear your brother's nappy."

Going home I was embarrassed –
It showed on my face,
Till my mum said, "Nobody knows
What's under your dress."

And the moral of my tale is this:
You can wear a smile –
Nobody knows what's underneath!

The Fun of Riots

It was time for school.
Two soldiers appeared at the door
And escorted us to the waiting truck.
Once on, we set off.

The Egyptian mobs threw rotten veg,
And we threw it back.
It was great fun!
Going to school during the riots.

Naturally, our parents didn't think so,
And, sadly, the day came
When we moved to Cyprus
To await our move back to England.

There was no school, but a holiday –
Swimming and just playing every day
Until the time came for us to leave,
Back to England, and into Nissen huts.

But best of all was no school –
They didn't have enough space for us.
It was cold in the hut, but we didn't mind
Dressing in coats and gloves
And playing snakes and ladders.

Good Old Mr W!

In our maths lesson, Mr W would say,
"Everyone write down one to ten."
(I'm sure you'll remember doing that?)
So we'd all write one to ten.

Then the questions would begin:
Question No. 1, and I'd put – ;
Question No. 2, and I'd put – ;
And so I'd continue through to No. 10.

But No. 10 was my question:
"Right then," Mr W would say,
"This one is especially for Pamela;
The rest of you don't need to bother,
For you'll only get it wrong!"

Then he'd say,
"If cabbages have four pence off,
How much are tuppenny bars of chocolate?"
And I'd write 'two pence'.

Whilst the rest of the class –
Just as he said, they got it wrong.
They were being just a bit too clever,
For they tried to work it out
By using percentages!
Mr W was my maths saviour!

My Hands and Feet

Now some folks can pat their head
And rub their tummy at the same time
(Or is it the other way round?),
But I never could do two things together.

So when it came to learning how to treadle
On the sewing machine at school,
I just couldn't master it,
Even though I tried three times.

And each time I took it up to the teacher
She'd say, "Go and try again."
And I'd unpick it and queue up again
To use the treadle machine.

Only to be told again,
"Go and try again,"
Till finally I'd had enough
And there were no machines to spare.

So I threaded a needle with cotton,
And I sewed a lovely straight line.
I took it up to show the teacher.
"Well done," she said.
"You've mastered it at last."

And I've never forgotten
That I can sew better
Than a sewing machine!

The Fancy Dress

Now, I've always had thick hair,
So getting it to stand up on end is easy;
And when we had a fancy-dress competition,
A golliwog was the obvious choice.

Now, nobody ever told me
That you're meant to put cream
Underneath the shoe polish
So that it comes off easily.

So there I was in the fancy-dress competition,
Looking like a gollywog with my hair stood up,
Black face, ears, neck and hands;
And I WON!

At twelve years old, you can imagine,
I was ecstatic with the applause
And the prize of a bar of chocolate;
But my happiness was short-lived.

I suddenly realised that I'd got just half an hour
Before I needed to be scrubbed and changed
Into my school uniform (clean blouse and all)
And seated in a confirmation class!

So there I sat in the class, most conspicuous,
With a scrubbed red face –
Neck, ears and hands still blackened –
In a clean white blouse that looked decidedly grubby!

I didn't learn much that night.
I knew I looked a sight,
And I only got through the evening
By fondling the bar of chocolate
That was waiting in my pocket!

The Washing

'Pamela won't ask,'
My school reports said.
It was the same at home,
So the end was always
Disaster!

When I was thirteen,
Mum went into hospital
And I tackled the chores.
The first was the washing.

The bits and pieces
Were kept in the cellar –
The copper boiler, the mangle
And the washing line.

Everything was fine
With the actual washing,
The mangle and the line,
Until I emptied the boiler!

It emptied through a tap,
So I turned it on:
The water ran into the drain,
Down to the tap level.

Then I heaved up the boiler
And, completely out of control,
It rolled across the floor.
Water went everywhere!

Including over the car battery
Charging up in the corner!
My dad was furious –
"Why didn't you ask?"

He said to leave it to him.
That was the first and the last
Time that I did the washing,
But Dad didn't get it as clean
As I did!

Little Snippets

We went gathering blackberries
With a ladder.
Of course, the inevitable happened
And we went home
All scratched and bloodied!

I thought that chocolate eclairs
Would be a nice change for tea,
So I set to with the recipe;
But I didn't understand the method.

The outer mixture was OK;
The problem was the filling:
"Put the sugar and margarine
Into a bag."

So I put it into a PAPER BAG!
Pipe with a paper bag? But how?
So it ended up
Hidden high up in the cupboard!

But when it came to
My little brother,
My mothering instinct
Really came up trumps.

He attended kindergarten,
Where he learnt, in English,
Counting and nursery rhymes,
Including 'Five Currant Buns'.

But most remembered was
When it was Parents' Day:
He was in the play
When he got all overwhelmed.

"Pamela!" he screamed,
As he ran from the platform.
I ran to get him
And gave him a cuddle
Before I took him home,
Loving each moment,
Despite the tear in my eye.

My Two Left Feet

"Fix my eyes on you, oh God –
That way I won't trip over my own two feet."
I read it in the psalms just recently,
But I wish I'd known about it long ago.

Like when I struggled with two left feet
In marching practice at college.
"Left, left, left," I heard –
But how to take a right in between?

Much to the amusement of the other cadets,
I practised with a postcard on my back.
"Please don't expect me to keep in step –
It's hard enough just to keep in line."

But it wasn't just me that got it wrong,
For to the back and the sides of me
Others were also consequently out of step.
How was I to manage the steps at the Albert Hall?

Then somebody figured out that,
Since there were ninety-nine cadets in our session,
One of us would need to march on their own;
And that one could be me!

This honour was bestowed on me
And the important day went well,
With only those behind me
Now out of step as well!

The Pen

I'd had a bit of a breakdown,
And was staying with my sister and family,
Looking after my nephew whilst they were at work –
Although really we looked after each other.

That particular morning
He came in, wanting a pen.
We searched but couldn't find one;
There wasn't an easy solution.

"Couldn't we go to the shop?" he asked.
"I'm sorry," I told him,
"I can't go into shops."
"And I can't go across the road," he answered,
Before he ran off to play again.

A few minutes later he was back.
"I've got a good idea:
If you take me across the road,
Then I'll take you in the shop."

And that's just what we did,
Which just goes to show
That a problem shared
Really is a problem halved.

In Our Little Westminster Hall

In our little Westminster hall
We had it all;
It's just that it had deteriorated!

We had a kitchen in which to cook,
But it always took two of us:
One to cook, and one to hold a brolly
To stop the rain dripping onto the stove
Through the hole in the ceiling!

We had a loo, but it leaked;
So when we flushed, a puddle spread
Across the loo floor and into the hall,
Right in front of the platform!

We had a caretaker too
Who'd clear up the mess whenever it happened,
Even if it was during the meeting
That someone had used the loo!
He'd fetch mop and bucket – it was soon sorted!

We also had a congregation –
Simple-minded but most sincere folk.
So what if they were poorly dressed?
They were always dressed clean and tidy.

So what if they did sing out of tune?
They were always loud enough
To be a good witness to anyone passing by.
They certainly knew how to praise the Lord.

Their testimonies were simple but so sincere –
Even if they did stand and say the same again.
So they said that last time,
But you knew it was true!

Just simple-minded folk –
But doesn't the Good Book say:
'That except you become as little children,
You shall in no wise enter the kingdom of heaven.'

We who consider ourselves as clever
Could learn a lot from them!

The Christenings

Both of my nephews were born
Within a few hours of each other.
They were born in the same ward,
And both had the same surname.

When my mum went to visit she said,
"Can I see Mrs Quinn and Mrs Quinn?"
The flustered nurse said, "I suppose
That you're Mrs Quinn as well?"
And my mum said, "That's right."

But they weren't a bit alike:
One was placid and contented,
Whilst the other was so lively
That we had difficulty in holding him.

We had a double christening
In an old village church.
As a family, we stood, each
Holding a candle as we watched.

The vicar took the lively one first;
He dribbled the water over the forehead,
But no one had noticed the baby's hand –
It was dipped in the font.

Up came the baby's hand and splashed –
The vicar was so wet that I really thought
He'd have to give the baby back
Whilst he went to get changed!

We were most amused,
But the vicar merely smiled
As he took the second baby,
Who, of course, was christened without
Mishap – as was his nature.

Three Answers to Prayer

Yes, that's right – three answers to prayer!
And all on a Friday morning
When I was seated behind my bookstall
At our Welcome In Café.

I answered my mobile phone to the words,
"Your prayers have been answered;
I'm phoning you from work;
I've got my job back. Isn't it great?"

I was just thanking the Lord for this answer
When in came another of our helpers.
"Do you know what happened to me yesterday?"
She asked. I shook my head.

"Well, yesterday I got locked out.
I'd left my keys in the house.
The phone was ringing and I knew it was my son;
We had agreed that he would ring me.

The phone stopped ringing and I saw an open window.
Well, I've never left a window open before,
And, just as I was climbing in, the phone rang again.
I answered it – it was my son."

During that five minutes between phone calls,
He had stopped to pray. He was concerned about me.
Where was I? Was I all right?
That was at the same time as I saw the open window.

So that was the second answer.
Off I went into the kitchen to share the news
And to get a much needed cuppa.
That was when someone else spoke up.

"On the way here I met my neighbour.
She told me that earlier on this week
She'd had a fall and couldn't see anyone around.
She prayed and a man appeared from around the corner.
He not only helped her up,
But he also saw her safely home."

Well, all I can say is,
"Isn't God great?"

Good Old British Rail!

Yes, that's right,
I'm praising British Rail –
I believe in credit where it's due –
When I needed it, they helped.

There I lay, half-naked,
Huddled on the platform.
The train left the station
And a railwayman approached me.

He assessed the situation and said,
"Just a minute, I'll fetch a blanket."
I followed him, now in the blanket,
Into his office.

There I sat drinking tea
And getting over the shock.
I had been sexually assaulted
Whilst two others watched!

They could have pulled the cord,
But the old man was protecting his wife.
When we came into the station
I managed to fall out of the door.

"Do you want to report this?"
He enquired. I shook my head.
I had coped with enough,
And settled for some more tea.

The train was stopped,
My luggage was taken off,
The criminal was escorted
To his destination.

In privacy I dressed again,
Boarded the next train
And continued on my journey,
With the support of a railwayman.

And so I say again,
"Good old British Rail!"
And God bless you,
Each and every one.

A Holiday with a Difference

Our host met us with a torch
And guided us from motor boat to caravan,
Provided us with half a loaf and a jug of milk,
Before exhausted we settled for the night.

The next morning we knocked at her door.
"Where do we get more milk?" we asked.
"You just help yourself," she replied.
"Where from?" came our puzzled question.

"Well," she said, "you see the cows and the goats?
You just help yourself," she repeated.
But neither of us knew anything about milking,
So we lived on powdered milk from the shop.

The post office was the only shop on the island,
And everything, large or small, tin or packet,
Weekly newspaper, a phone call –
Everything – cost just (or as much as) £1!

Around the island was just one road,
With the only car belonging to the district nurse.
There were no trees – it was far too windy –
And the weekly wash was weighted down by large stones.

Why did they risk putting out the washing
Whilst the cows and the goats freely trampled on it?
And how did they manage to earn a living
When all we could see was caravans wired up to houses?

Everyone on the island spoke Gaelic,
But when they saw us, they politely said,
"Good day, our English visitors."
The children learnt in Gaelic until they were twelve years old.

Then they continued their education in English
Whilst they boarded, weekly, on the mainland.
On the Sunday we joined everyone else
At the church and were made welcome in Gaelic!

Very bravely we attempted to join in the worship,
Struggling to bob up and down in the right places.
The only musical accompaniment was from a little man
Who stood and sang the first line. Then they all joined in.

The praying and the singing all came from the Psalms;
But 'twas all in Gaelic and we only knew English.
Thankfully, when it came to the sermon we were spared
As we heard, "Welcome. Our sermon will be in English."

This was certainly a holiday with a difference:
Two and a half days' travel from Glasgow, where I worked,
And even further for my friend, who was working in Belfast,
But long to be remembered – this island in the Outer Hebrides!

The Fireside Companions

Now, normally speaking,
Mum would know when they were coming
(My sister-in-law and my nephew),
And away behind her chair
Would go the fireside companion set.

But on this particular occasion
They caught us quite by surprise,
And the first thing my nephew spied
Was the fireside companion set,
Sitting there unnoticed – or so we thought,
But he'd seen it.

He walked towards it and we held our breath.
With a solemn look, he picked up the little shovel
And handed it to his gran,
Who, with a straight face,
Placed it behind her chair.

Piece by piece
He gave them to Gran,
And straight-faced she put them
Behind her chair.

We smiled but we dare not laugh,
For here was a little child showing us
That if you can't avoid temptation
Then hide it from your sight –
A lesson we could all do with learning!

What Was He Wearing?

I had only been using sign language for a few weeks
When into our evening church service
Came my deaf friend with such a sad face.
Naturally I asked, "What's the matter?"

I thought she told me,
"Kevin is missing on his bike."
"When did you last see him?"
She hadn't seen her husband since the previous night.

'She must be worried sick,' I thought to myself,
So I signalled to the assistant church officer.
Over he came, and in a whisper I explained
Before all three of us trooped out of the church.

Once in the office, we rang the police station,
And there followed a four-way conversation
Between the policeman and Stuart, who were speaking,
And my deaf friend and I, who were signing.

On and on until the final question:
"What was he wearing?"
Back came the answer:
"The bike is green." Light dawned.

It wasn't Kevin on his bike that was missing;
It was "Kevin's bike is missing!"
It was quite a while before I lived that one down.

My Mum's Home

I visited my mum's home in Cumberland
And stayed with her Aunty Dolly.
She wasn't really Mum's aunty,
But her next-door neighbour,
Who'd looked after her and the twins
When her own mum had died
And her dad was out to work.

But a real smile comes about
When I remember that first day:
I had been sent on a 'message'
To the corner shop for bread.
It took me three hours!

For every time I passed a window
Somebody would run out and say,
"Come away in, our Mary's daughter,"
And I'd follow them into their house
And spend an hour or so
Telling them about Mum and the family!

Aunty Dolly's house was different:
The cooking was done on the coal fire,
Or in one of the ovens placed at either side.
In bed I had a stone hot-water bottle.

The bath was under the kitchen table!
It was filled with water boiled on the fire,
And of course the whole family
Used the one lot of water.

Now, all that was an adventure,
But it was the outside toilet
That I hated – so cold and uninviting!
Thankfully, at night I could
Use the 'chatty' kept under the bed.

Me and Mine

It was just before Christmas
And I was absolutely broke,
Having sent a large parcel off to my family
Of everything I thought they'd like.

I was working in Scotland –
Dundee, to be exact –
And due to take my Christmas leave
In the following January.

But how to afford the train fare?
That was the problem.
But it wasn't a problem for very long,
For it's like the Good Book says:
"Cast your bread upon the waters
And it will not come back to you void."

My present from my family
Was my train fare!
So I had two Christmases
And the best of both worlds:
Christmas with the kids that I loved,
And a second Christmas
With my own family!

Laughing at Your Mistakes

Most of us have mistaken salt for sugar:
I did it on a parents' day
When I was making shortbread;
But I've also put
Milk in cola, thinking it was tea.

Have you ever left the keys hanging on the door?
Did you get locked in?
I did whilst working in a remand home,
And it took two hours to get me out
Because the staff needed to follow the clues
To the keys that were attached to the dog's collar!

Did you ever set out to do a favour and it went wrong?
I offered to get a railway ticket – to Abber something –
But when I got to the ticket office
The queue was so long that I amused myself
By reading through all the other names beginning with Abber!
Consequently, when I got to the ticket office
I blurted out, "I need a ticket to Abber-what's-it."

And how are you at your Scottish?
I asked the taxi driver to take me to Edinburgh Georgie
When I should have pronounced it Gorgie!
And how do you cope with being scared?
On a Belfast Army platform I said,
"We're going to use the tune 'Londonderry Air' –
I hope you know it!"

And those are only some of my laughs! –
I bet you've got many more.

'Happy Get Rid of It' Day!

Just one day in the whole year?
Okay, if you need a bit of a jolt;
But surely life with Jesus means
Every day is my
'Happy Get Rid of It' Day.

For the Lord is my shredding machine –
Throughout 2007 I proved it to be,
Constantly coming to Him again and again.
Shredding – our talks got priorities sorted out.
He led me beside quiet waters
When I was overwhelmed,
Feelings top heavy, and unsure of my way.
He calmed my fears;
I knew that all would be well.

He guided me in paths of righteousness.
I planned a holiday to Canada
To visit Abigail, who couldn't talk.
I laid out the difficulties before the Lord:
I had the wrong address and no phone number;
I'd never been so far away on my own before.
I left it all with Him – no worries! Jesus would sort it.
A miracle was all mine when I arrived:
Abigail stared up into my face and said,
"Hi, Pam – miss you."

*Yea, though I walk through
The valley of the shadow of death –*
This was the year that I lost loved ones.

Lord, You shredded it up,
Carried me through one step at a time;
Your rod and your staff they comfort me.
You gave me, Lord, such support from friends.
I never knew prayer could uphold one so;
And underneath are the everlasting arms.

You prepared a table before me,
But before I could feast I needed to learn –
Maybe it was patience?
I just know that others despaired, and me.
From August to December:
A phone gremlin lived at No. 33.
Continually I brought it to the powers that be;
But it's working now –
Honestly! Ring me and see!

My cup runneth over.
This was difficult to accept at first;
Losing loved ones left a big hole in my life.
I stood, staring up at the Cross, and Jesus said to me,
"Daughter, behold your mother;
Woman, behold your son."
I was – I am – still needed in this world.

Surely goodness and mercy shall follow me
All the days of my life.
For each day will be – nay, each moment
Will be – my 'Happy Get Rid of It',
For *the Lord is my Shepherd*,
And with this I'm more than content!

Amusement and Encouragement

As I come to the close of this little book,
Memories of friends and friendships crowd my mind.
Some are far too personal to share,
Whilst others just beg to be shared.

I remember with amusement
My most recent tutor
Singing and signing, "Wild thing, I love ye,"
And her gift to me when she told me,
"You are my most promising student."

I remember Auntie Elsie (as known by one and all)
Who, whilst well into her nineties,
Dreamt about Scrabble letters and moves;
And many a time when coming down to breakfast
She'd tell us that if you had such and such a letter
And you landed on a coloured square,
What a total you would get!

As I've moved around the country,
I've had so many 'surrogate mums'
And people who have been like big sisters to me;
And their home has become my home.
Whenever I have been 'off duty'
It's been just great to relax with them.

And finally, for the encouragement of friends
Who have helped me change
My "I can't" into "I can!" – thank you.